LIGHTNING BOLT BOOKS™

Ew, Reptiles!

India James

Lerner Publications ◆ Minneapolis

To Johnny, Natasha, and Aiden

Lerner Publications Company
An imprint of Lerner Publishing Group, Inc.
241 First Avenue North
Minneapolis, MN 55401 USA

For reading levels and more information, look up this title at www.lernerbooks.com.

Main body text set in Billy Infant Regular. Typeface provided by SparkyType.

Editor: Nicole Berglund **Photo Editor:** Nicole Berglund
Lerner team: Sue Marquis

Library of Congress Cataloging-in-Publication Data

Names: James, India, author.
Title: Ew, reptiles! / India James.
Description: Minneapolis : Lerner Publications, [2026] | Series: Lightning bolt books—creepy creatures | Includes bibliographical references and index. | Audience: Ages 6-9. | Audience: Grades 2-3. | Summary: "Reptiles slither and crawl, and some even have sharp teeth! Readers explore different types of spooky reptiles, including the pig-nosed turtle and the frilled lizard"— Provided by publisher.
Identifiers: LCCN 2024039730 (print) | LCCN 2024039731 (ebook) | ISBN 9798765669020 (library binding) | ISBN 9798765684634 (paperback) | ISBN 9798765679814 (epub)
Subjects: LCSH: Reptiles—Miscellanea—Juvenile literature.
Classification: LCC QL644.2 .J36 2026 (print) | LCC QL644.2 (ebook) | DDC 597.9—dc23/eng/20240930

LC record available at https://lccn.loc.gov/2024039730
LC ebook record available at https://lccn.loc.gov/2024039731

Manufactured in the United States of America
1-1011581-53873-11/20/2024

Table of Contents

Weird!

Whoosh! Something long and black glides through the sky. It looks like a flying snake!

Some people think reptiles are creepy. They have scales or big teeth. But reptiles can be fun to discover. Let's learn about some spooky reptiles!

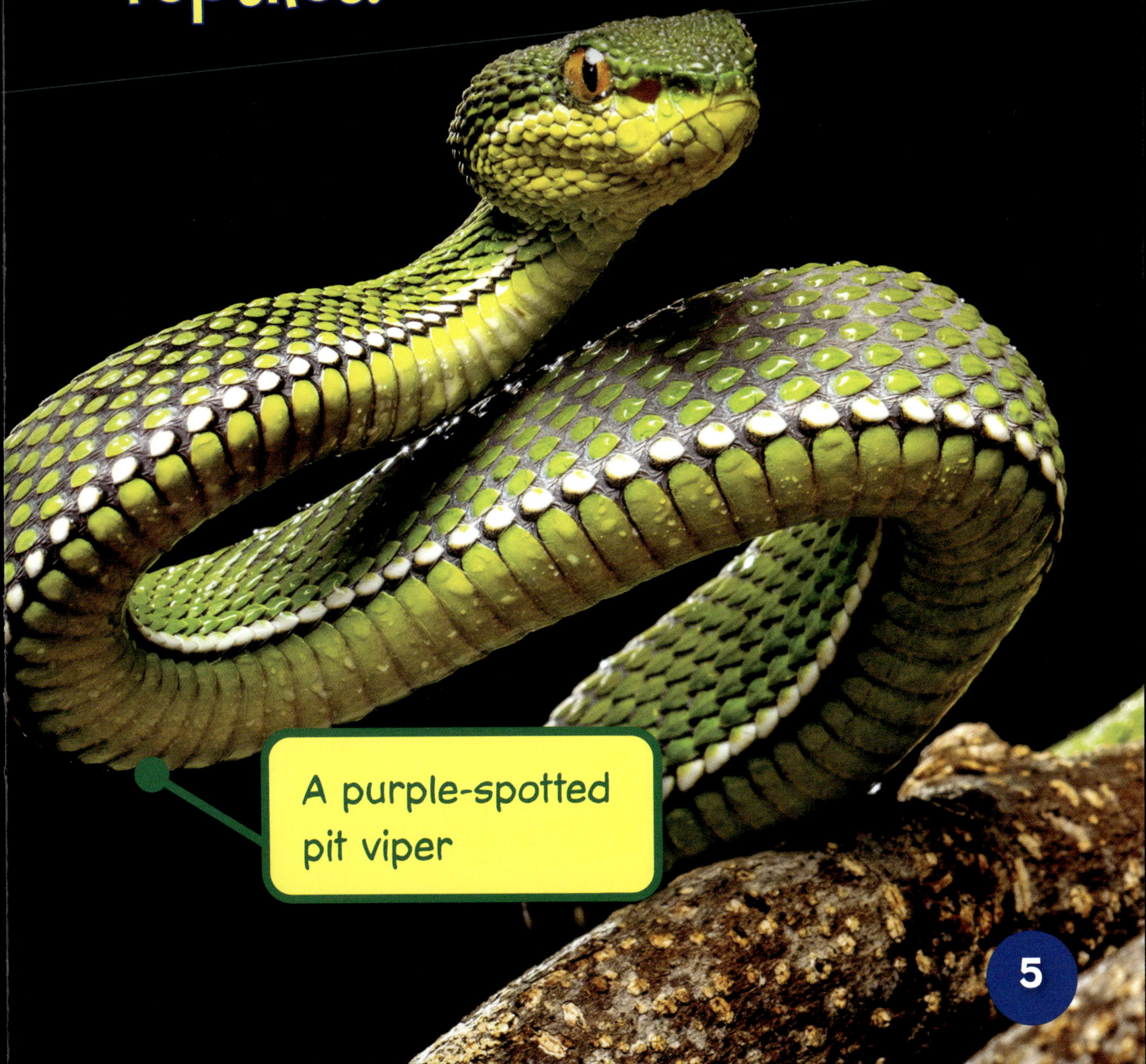

A purple-spotted pit viper

Super Reptiles

The paradise tree snake is green, red, yellow, and black. It can blend in with flowers on trees. But it can also glide through the air!

A paradise tree snake jumps through the air.

Before it jumps, the paradise tree snake flattens its body. Then it leaps and glides to another tree. This helps it reach food such as lizards and birds.

The frilled lizard has a special way of scaring off predators. It opens its mouth wide and flips out a frill of skin around its head.

Frilled lizards eat bugs and small lizards.

Most frilled lizards live in Australia.

In some areas the frilled lizard is called a frilled dragon. Its frill makes it look like a dragon from a fairy tale.

Gharials hatch from their eggs within eighty days.

The gharial has a long, thin snout with up to 110 teeth.

Its eggs are the largest of any crocodile species.

Gharials are great swimmers, but they don't move well on land. Instead of walking, they push themselves forward on their bellies.

Is it a pig? Is it a turtle? The pig-nosed turtle looks like both!

This turtle's nose sticks out from the front of its head. The nostrils make it look like a pig. Its nose helps it breathe underwater.

The spiny bush viper has spiky scales covering its body. If you see it, stay away! This snake's venom can harm humans.

The spiny bush viper can be many colors. Its rough, pointy scales can be yellow, green, blue, or brown.

The spiny bush viper lives in Africa.

A turtle with bright green hair? No way! Some Mary River turtles look as if they are from a cartoon.

The Mary River turtle doesn't actually have hair. Green algae sometimes grow on the top of its head. **This can help it hide from predators.**

Scaly and Sharp

Many reptiles have scales or spikes. Some reptiles have sharp teeth. These features make reptiles look spooky!

Scales, spikes, and sharp teeth are a warning to stay away. Reptiles are amazing creatures to watch and learn about. What do you think? Are reptiles spooky?

Spooky or Cute?

The panther chameleon can turn its skin any color. And its tongue can unroll to be longer than its body! Can you decide if this reptile is spooky or cute?

Reptile Facts

- Some lizards can remove their tails to escape if caught by a predator.
- Horned lizards can squirt blood from their eyes to defend themselves.
- Basilisk lizards can run on water.
- Aldabra tortoises can live more than 150 years. They're some of the longest-living animals on Earth.

Glossary

algae: types of plants that grow in water

frill: a fold of skin or tissue around an animal's neck

nostril: an opening on the nose

predator: an animal that hunts other animals for food

scale: one of the hard plates that cover and protect a reptile's skin

snout: the part of an animal's head that sticks out and contains the nose and jaws

venom: poison that some animals make and use to hurt other animals

Learn More

Britannica Kids: Reptiles
https://kids.britannica.com/students/article/reptiles/276696

Emminizer, Theresa. *Slithering Snakes*. Buffalo: Enslow, 2024.

Golusky, Jackie. *Saltwater Crocodiles: Nature's Biggest Reptile*. Minneapolis: Lerner Publications, 2024.

Humphrey, Natalie. *It's a Reptile!* Buffalo: Gareth Stevens, 2025.

National Geographic Kids: Reptiles
https://kids.nationalgeographic.com/animals/reptiles

NeoK12: Reptiles
https://www.neok12.com/Reptiles.htm

Index

Photo Acknowledgments

Image credits: Cede Prudente/Getty Images, p. 4; dlewis33/Getty Images, p. 5; blickwinkel/Alamy, p. 6; Cede Prudente/NHPA/Photoshot/Science Source, p. 7; Ken Griffiths/Alamy, p. 8; Heru Agung/Getty Images, p. 9; johntallboy/Shutterstock, p. 10; Milan Zygmunt/500px/Getty Images, p. 11; Paulo Resende/Shutterstock, p. 12; daniilphotos/Shutterstock, p. 13; Mark_Kostich/Shutterstock, p. 14; Nature Picture Library/Alamy, p. 15; Photography by Rob D/Shutterstock, pp. 16-17; Roberto Dani/500px/Getty Images, p. 18; Buena Vista Images/Getty Images, p. 19; kuritafsheen/Getty Images, p. 20.

Cover: Mark Kostich/Getty Images.